animal babies
in grasslands

KINGFISHER

Kingfisher Publications Plc
New Penderel House
283–288 High Holborn
London WC1V 7HZ
www.kingfisherpub.com

First published by Kingfisher Publications Plc 2004

2 4 6 8 10 9 7 5 3 1

RH/0704/TWP/PICA(PICA)/150STORA

A CIP catalogue record for this book is
available from the British Library.

0 7534 0943 7

Author and Editor: Jennifer Schofield
Designer: Joanne Brown
Jacket Design: Joanne Brown
Picture Manager: Cee Weston-Baker
Picture Researcher: Rachael Swann
DTP Manager: Nicky Studdart
Senior Production Controller: Deborah Otter

Printed in Singapore

animal babies

in grasslands

I have big **ears** and a long **nose** called a trunk.
I use my **trunk** to spray myself with **water**.

Who is my mummy?

My mummy is an elephant and I am her calf.

When it is hot, my mummy and I walk to the river. We like to play in the water to keep cool.

My tail is like a paintbrush. It swishes from side to side to keep the flies off my black and white stripes.

Who is my mummy?

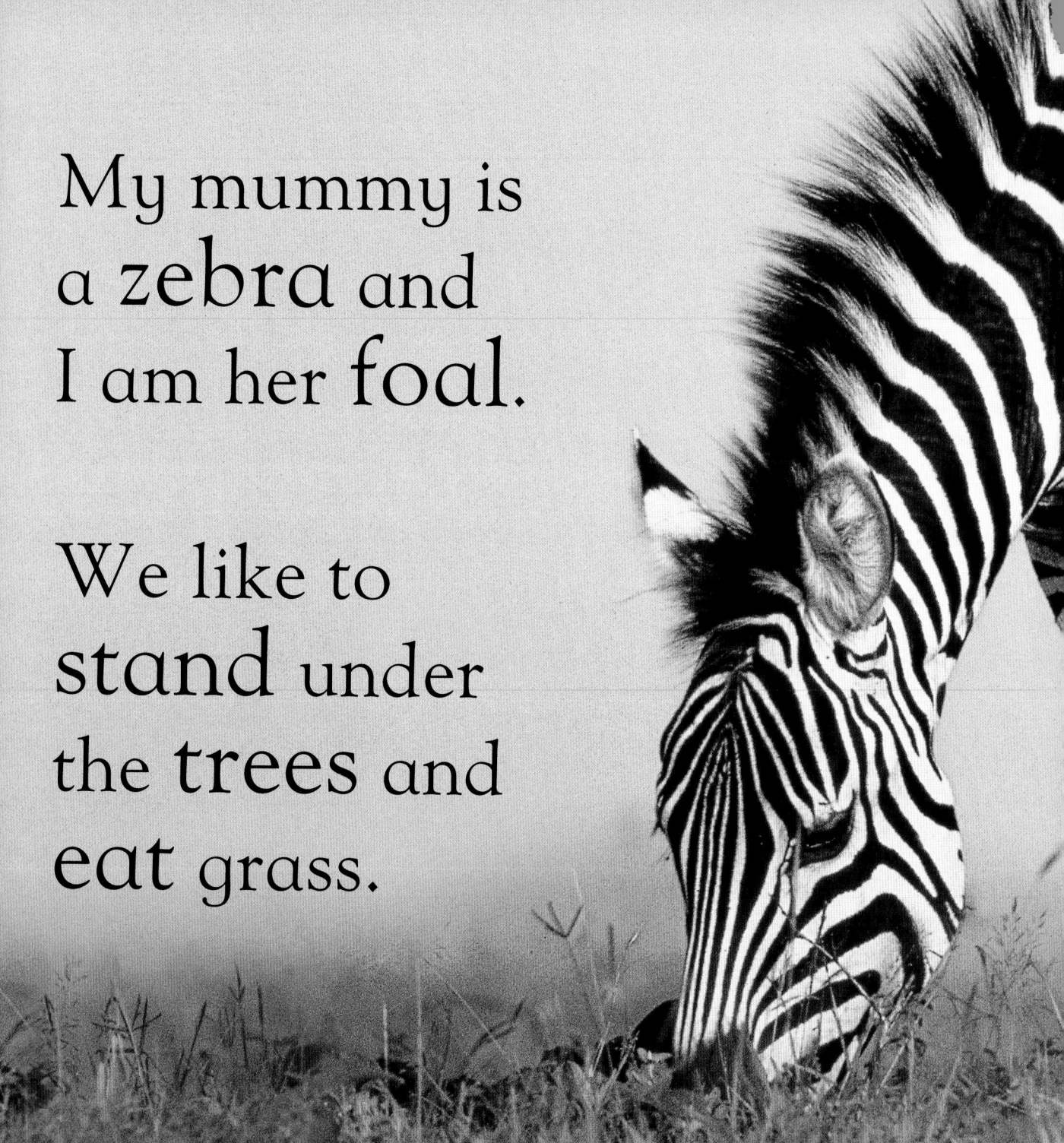

My mummy is a zebra and I am her foal.

We like to stand under the trees and eat grass.

When I am **older**, I will **roar** so loudly that you can **hear** me from **far** away.

Who is my mummy?

My mummy is a lion
and I am her cub.

I play with my
mummy when she
is not hunting
for our food.

I am small and furry. My little tail has a black tip. When trouble is near, I bark very loudly.

Who is my mummy?

My mummy is a prairie dog and I am her pup.

We like to play in the warm sunshine, but we go underground to sleep at night.

My mummy has a pouch on her tummy. When I am cold, I sit in the pouch to keep warm.

Who is my mummy?

My mummy is a kangaroo and I am her joey.

Walking takes too long, so we hop very quickly from place to place.

I have the longest neck of all animals. It helps me to reach leaves on the tops of very tall trees.

Who is my mummy?

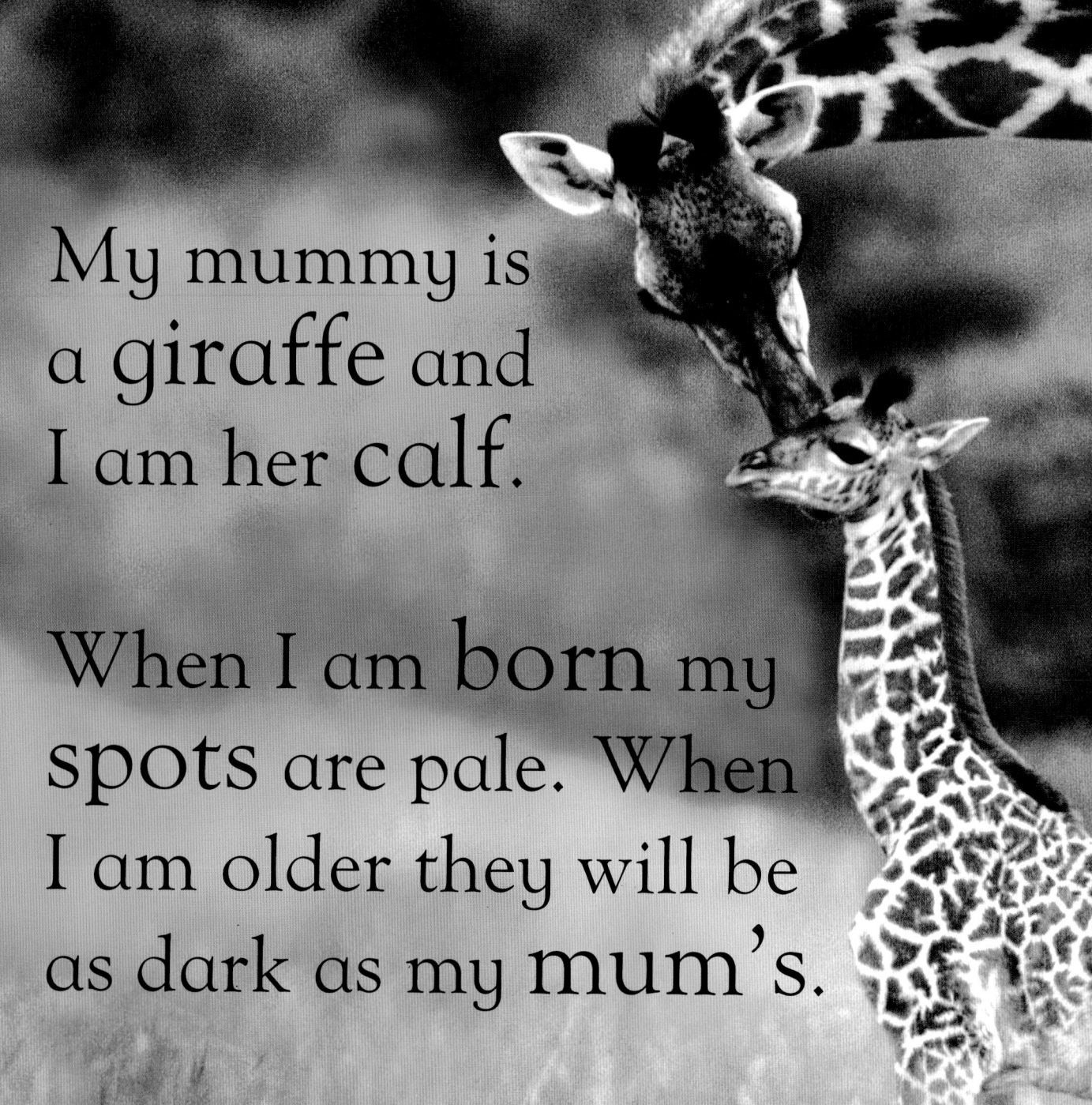

My mummy is
a giraffe and
I am her calf.

When I am born my
spots are pale. When
I am older they will be
as dark as my mum's.

The **rings** around my eyes look like **sunglasses**. They **help** me to watch out for dangerous **animals**.

Who is my mummy?

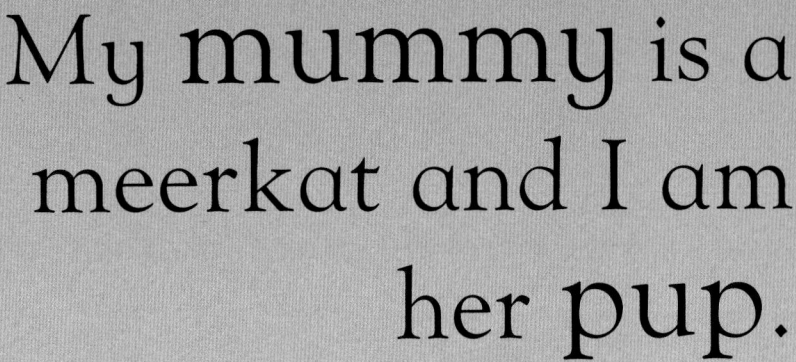

My mummy is a meerkat and I am her pup.

My family is called a gang and we live in a burrow underground.

Additional Information

Almost one-quarter of the earth's land area is grassland. There are many different words for grassland environments around the world, including savannahs, pampas, campos, plains, steppes, prairies and veldts. The animals in this book are found in various regions: elephants, zebras, lions, giraffes and meerkats are found in the hot and dry savannah of Africa; kangaroos are found in the Australian outback; and, as their name suggests, prairie dogs are found in the Prairies of North America.

Acknowledgements

The publisher would like to thank the following for permission to reproduce their material. Every care has been taken to trace copyright holders. However, if there have been unintentional omissions or failure to trace copyright holders, we apologise and will, if informed, endeavour to make corrections in any future edition.

Cover: Caesar Lucas Abreu/Imagebank/Getty; Half title: Ferrero Labat/Ardea; Title page: Clem Haagner/Ardea; Elephant 1: Tony Heald/NaturePL; Elephant 2: Martin Harvey/Alamy Images; Zebra 1: Ferrero Labat/Ardea; Zebra 2: Ferrero Labat/Ardea; Lion 1: Caesar Lucas Abreu/Imagebank/Getty; Lion 2: Jean-Marc Treuchet/Stone/Getty; Prairie dog 1: M Chillmaid/Oxford Scientific Films; Prairie dog 2: Gail Shumway/Taxi/Getty; Kangaroo 1: Jean Paul Ferrero/Ardea; Kangaroo 2 Jean Paul Ferrero/Ardea; Giraffe 1: M. Watson/Ardea; Giraffe 2: K&K Ammann/Taxi/Getty; Meerkat 1: T Jackson/Oxford Scientific Films; Meerkat 2: Clem Haagner/Ardea